Science Sight Word Readers™

Octopuses and Squid

by Max Andover

ISBN 978-0-545-24792-4

Photographs © 2011: cover: Nature Picture Library Ltd./Jeff Rotman; back cover top: iStockphoto/John Anderson; back cover bottom, page 1: Photo Researchers, NY/Novastock; page 2: Getty Images/David Fleetham/Visuals Unlimited, Inc.; page 3: Alamy Images/Reinhard Dirscherl; page 4: Nature Picture Library Ltd./Jeff Rotman; page 5: Minden Pictures/Fred Bavendam; page 6: Seapics.com/John C. Lewis; page 7: Alamy Images/Jeff Rotman; page 8: Photo Researchers, NY/British Antarctic Survey; page 9: Seapics.com/Bob Cranston; page 10: Getty Images/Brian Skerry; page 11: Seapics.com/Franco Banfi; page 12 top: Seapics.com/Miami/e-Photography; page 12 bottom left: Photo Researchers, NY/Dante Fenolio; page 12 bottom right: Photo Researchers, NY/Zafer Kizilkaya; page 13 top left: Photo Researchers, NY/Dante Fenolio; page 13 top right: Photo Researchers, NY/F. Stuart Westmorland; page 13 bottom: Seapics.com/John C. Lewis; page 14: Photo Researchers, NY/Dante Fenolio; page 15: iStockphoto/Island Effects; page 16: iStockphoto/PlanctonVideo.

Photo research by Jenna Addesso; Design by Holly Grundon

SCHOLASTIC INC.

NEW YORK • TORONTO • LONDON • AUCKLAND
SYDNEY • MEXICO CITY • NEW DELHI • HONG KONG

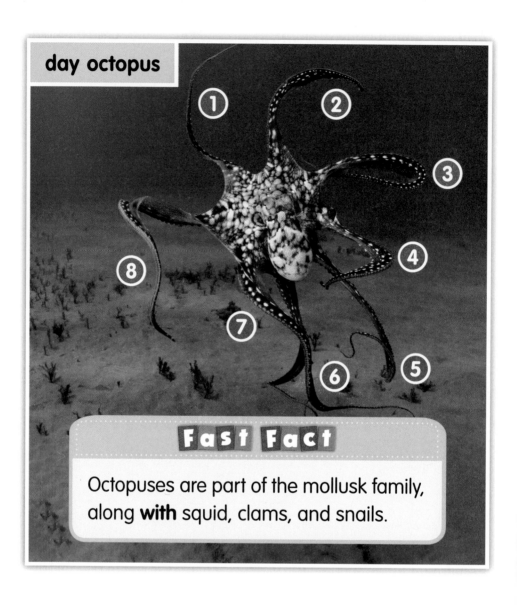

day octopus

① ② ③ ④ ⑤ ⑥ ⑦ ⑧

Fast Fact

Octopuses are part of the mollusk family, along **with** squid, clams, and snails.

An octopus is a cool creature **with eight long arms!**

coconut octopus

Fast Fact

Octopuses have soft bodies and no backbones. This one hides in a shell.

It can squeeze its soft body into a very small space.

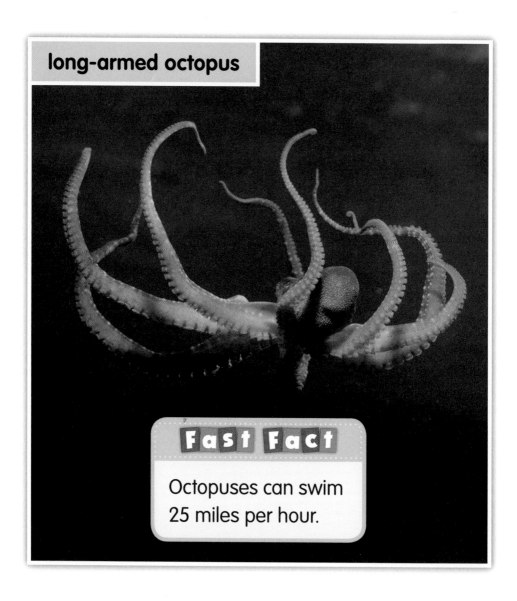

long-armed octopus

Fast Fact

Octopuses can swim 25 miles per hour.

An octopus is a cool creature **with eight long arms**! It can swim fast.

Fast Fact

Octopuses eat fish, crabs, turtles, and dead sharks.

It can use its **long arms** to grab food.

southern keeled octopus

Fast Fact

Some octopuses can change color to blend in **with** their surroundings.

An octopus is a cool creature **with eight long arms**! It can hide.

giant octopus

Fast Fact

Octopus predators include:
- moray eels
- dolphins
- whales
- sharks

It can squirt ink to scare away predators.

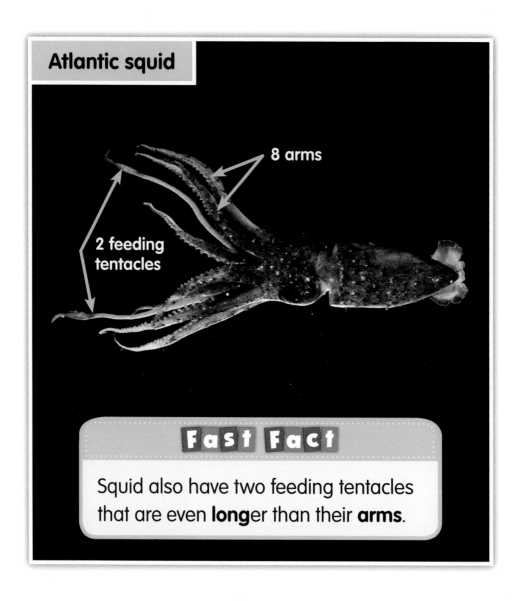

Atlantic squid

8 arms

2 feeding tentacles

Fast Fact

Squid also have two feeding tentacles that are even **long**er than their **arms**.

A squid is another cool creature **with eight long arms!**

Humboldt squid

Fast Fact

Squid eat fish, shrimp, and other squid.

It can use its **long arms** to grab and eat fish.

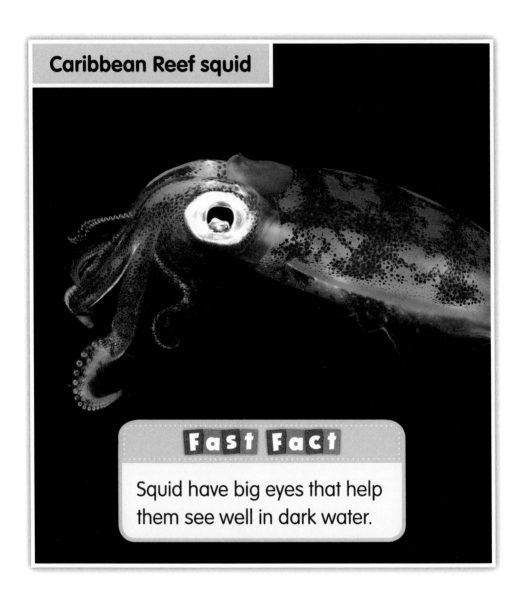

Caribbean Reef squid

Fast Fact

Squid have big eyes that help them see well in dark water.

A squid is a cool creature **with eight long arms**! It can see well.

Humboldt squid

Fast Fact

This kind of squid can be six feet **long**.

It can be huge!

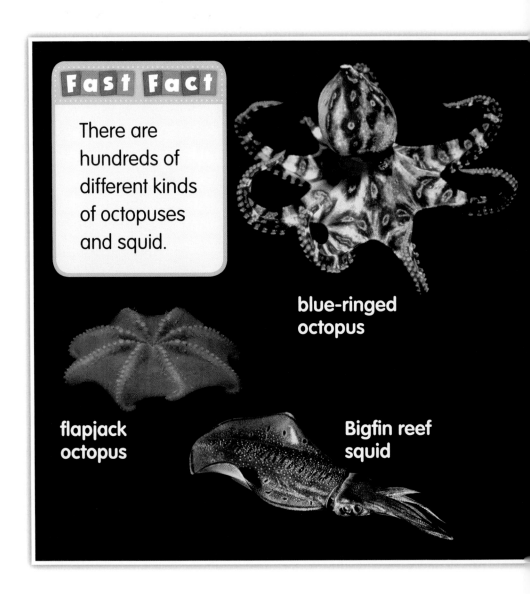

There are hundreds of different kinds of octopuses and squid.

blue-ringed octopus

flapjack octopus

Bigfin reef squid

Octopuses and squid are cool creatures **with eight long arms**.

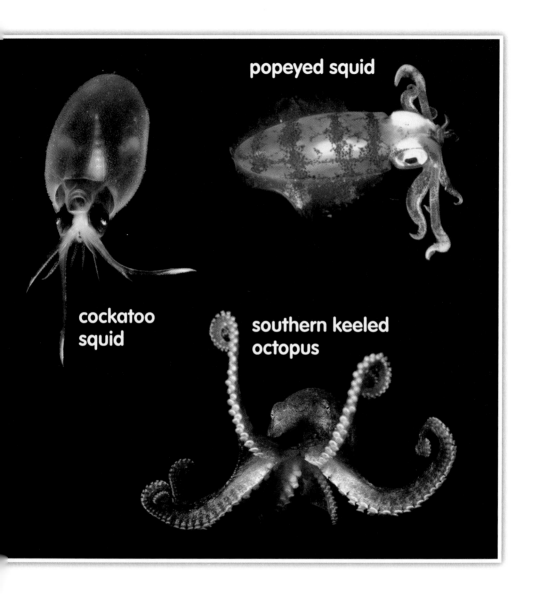

popeyed squid

cockatoo squid

southern keeled octopus

Clap your two hands for these amazing animals of the sea!

Sight Word Review

Point to each sight word. Then read it aloud.

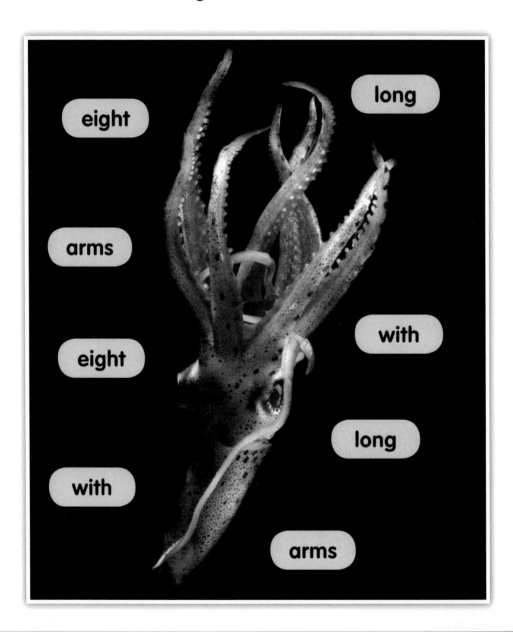

Sight Word Fill-ins

Use one sight word from the box to finish each sentence.

arms	eight
long	with

1. Squid chomp food _____ their birdlike beaks.

2. Octopuses have _____ arms.

3. Like octopuses and squid, you use your _____ every day.

4. Have you been learning about sea creatures for a _____ time?

All About
Octopuses and Squid

Ask a grown-up to read this with you.

Both octopuses and squid are mollusks. Clams, snails, and slugs are also mollusks. Mollusks don't have backbones.

Both octopuses and squid have eight arms. If they lose an arm, it grows back. Squid also have two feeding tentacles. Octopuses and squid move through the ocean in a very unusual way. They squirt water out of their bodies. This is called jet propulsion. Both octopuses and squid are poisonous. When they bite prey such as fish and shrimp with their sharp parrot-like beaks, they deliver a dose of venom.

There are some really big octopuses. The giant octopus can grow to more than 15 feet long from arm tip to arm tip. And there are some really big squid. A giant squid can grow to be over 50 feet long. Its eyes are the size of basketballs. Giant squid are rarely seen, but Japanese scientists were able to film one in 2006. The videotape will help them understand more about this rare and mysterious creature of the sea!